IMPROVE YOUR PEOPLE SKILLS

A GUIDEBOOK TO IMPROVE YOUR SOCIAL SKILLS, WIN FRIENDS, UNLEASH THE EMPATH IN YOU AND RAISE YOUR EMOTIONAL QUOTIENT

By Greg Williams

Table of Contents

Chapter 1: Social Skills

Definition of Social Skills

A social skill is an ability that helps one to interact as well as communicate with other persons. The skills can either be verbal or non-verbal, through gesture, personal appearance as well as body language. As well, social power is learned conduct that allows an individual to reach social reinforcement. Social skills are known to create as well as maintain relationships between people. They help us to initiate conversations, make friends, have excellent sportsmanship as well as be in a position to handle bullying efficiently. The process that we learn social skills is referred to as socialization. Some analysts prefer using the term behavioral skills In the place of social skills.

Behavioral skills help build social skills. The skills are used in treating addiction and also are a way of helping people who suffer from depression, developmental disabilities as well as indefinite personality disorders. Considering that people encounter numerous social problems, having an encounter in a safe environment will ease the stress as well as the punishment from the meeting. Helping one have the right social skills will raise their reinforcement. Social skills are linked to being successful, have independence as well as emotional well-being. Excellent social skills will help you demonstrate the superior potential to observe, solving problems as well as responding in social circumstances. Humans are a social being and pose social skills is a vital way to help them communicate with one another. We can communicate with others and deliver messages, what we are thinking and also what we feel. You need to have social skills to make a conversation successful.

Why Social Skills are Inside to All of Us

Everyone is supposed to be equipped with social skills to help them to run their day to day life. Consistency will not be achieved when we do not have the right social skills. Being regarded as a decent human being will come from one exercising their social powers in the expected ways. We all need to have excellent social skills despite age, gender, ethnicity, as well as our status. There are reasons why we have the social abilities inside of us. The reasons include.

To enable us to create more Relationships

Identifying with people will result in a relationship, and many cases end up in a friendship. You cannot grow in life if you do not recognize your relationship with other individuals. For you to find satisfaction in life, you need to have a social network that enables you to create new friends. Having social skills with us will help us to identify well with people, you become charismatic as well as have an admirable character. People like interacting with charismatic individuals because they seem to be interested in the other party. For you to advance in life, you will be required to have firm interpersonal relations with people. Excellent sharpened social skills will help you live a happy as well as a pleasant experience and give you a better view of life.

To promote excellent Communications

Social skills will develop your interaction with other persons since you can communicate with them. Having better communication skills will boost your social skills. We are able to deliver the thoughts as well as our ideas and what we generally fell. The reason we should have social skills in us is so that we can relate to people. We are also in a position to work in a big group. Communication can either be verbal or non-verbal. Non-verbal communication connects people and as well build trust between them. Making eye contact, occasionally nodding when talking with someone and maintaining an open posture indicates that you are not closed off. Having social skills in us is more than speaking typically but as well as integrating nonverbal skills.

To aid us in achieving more Efficiency

If you love interacting with people, you need to avoid being around the people you cannot be compatible with. Spending time with a person who has no similar interest as well as a viewpoint with you will not help grow. In such cases, you need to use a polite way to tell that person you need to find someone else to interact with. Possessing excellent social skills will help you know how to handle that person to achieve more efficiency. When in a social situation, you need to spend time with the people that you share some ideas and have similar intentions that will help you advance in life. Having a set of excellent social skills will always help you be polite in all situations. Learn to say no when you don't want to engage in something, and people will embrace that with time. Participating in a conversation when you feel not interested will kill your moral to participate in a productive talk.

Helping us to build a better Career

Working in any organizational set up will require you to have excellent social skills. You tend to spend more time interacting with either your colleagues or your employees. You cannot stay in isolation since that will not contribute to the success of the organization. The social skill that you have will help you have a healthy relationship in your workplace. Excellence, as well as growth, will be achieved when everyone brings together their unique talents. Getting along as well as understanding people will expose you to many career-related outlets. The social skills that you have will as well help you in some cases to secure a job. Even after securing the post, you will be more likely to make progress. Everyone appreciates good work, practicing social skills that you have will as well make you be promoted. Having excellent social skills will serve as a way of influencing as well as motivating people to have things done in the way they are supposed. Some conversations may even lead to you securing a well-paying job or a salary increment.

Improve your quality of Life

Social skills help us to create significant social networks that later help us to deal with loneliness or depression. You are likely to experience a happy being compared to someone who has no social networks or an introvert. Better social skills can help us to boost our confidence and strike a conversation with someone, which may lead to the creation of a friendship. Engaging in an interview will help you stay warm and comfortable too. It is essential and will help you live a long and healthy life. Social skills will serve as a foundation of a positive relationship with either your friend or family. You feel the sense of belonging when associated with a particular social get together. You can't compare living a timid life and being bold. Keeping much to your self will do more harm than good. Thinking positively will give other people the impression that you are fun and productive to be around with. With developed social skills, you get more confident with how you conduct yourself in either a social or professional setting.

To help you manage Conflicts

Developing social skills will help you better understand how people interact in any social setting. You will adapt to any personality and have the confidence to manage conflict in case of any. Having social skills will help you how to have a productive conversation to resolve disputes. You will learn how to listen as well as interpreting body language actively. It will aid you in knowing the kind of response to give.

It will benefit both you and the ones around you

You will not give yourself the chance to blend with people if you don't like to mingle with people in a social gathering. Being in a social group will help you boost your social life as well as the relationship. You will have a chance to meet with other persons besides the ones you know. Meeting new faces will allow you to interact with resourceful persons. The more you interact with different people, the higher the chances of growing. Knowing how and what makes people comfortable will be boosted by your social skills. Engaging in a conversation with someone can impact them positively, even without your knowledge. Your self-confidence will be increased, and you will not be afraid of making any errors. Having social skills in you will help you to know how to conduct yourself, whatever the case, and in any situation. Being enthusiastic makes your character attracts the people around you. That will give you an excellent opportunity to widen your circles as well as strengthening your relationships.

Why Social Skills are Affecting Our Lives

Even though social skills are viewed as tools to help the society, as well as individuals, grow, they can also affect us negatively. Poor social skills, as well as lack of these skills, will lead to increased cases of stress and depression. Your mental health, as well as the physical one, can be significantly harmed as a result. You are more likely to experience difficulties in handling other people as well as your relationships.

Some necessary social skills, like communication, have several effects on our lives. Poor communication skills will lead to the breaking of relationships as well as leads to arguments. You will lose the morale to do anything, and in an organizational set-up, this will lead to reduced turnover. Productivity is as well likely to go down, and hence, the desired results will not be achieved. Conflicts and disagreements will arise between people affecting how they relate with each other. Communication through modern technology can, at times lead to reduced sociability amongst people. It makes young people lack confidence and cannot deliver before a social gathering. Lack of trust will keep you away from a multitude of opportunities. Helping other people grow is our primary goal in life, and this may not come to be if we do not interact with people often. You may not know what people are going through and what their feelings are if you don't get to socialize with them. The advantages associated with having the desired social skills may not accompany someone who has no appropriate social skills. Lacking social skills will be difficult for you to make it in life.

Being an introvert will result in loneliness, which leads to stressful situations, and it may grow to be depression. Not meeting with people on a regular basis can keep you away from many job opportunities. Using your social skills in a recommendable way can make your career growth and vice versa. Some social skills can lead to someone being proud. Pride will make one not want to interact with someone of a different financial level with them. It will make them feel avoided, and that may lead them to seclude themselves and fell avoided too. Downcast eyes are, in some cases, viewed as someone being shy or lack confidence. It is as well regarded as a sign of indecency in some cultural practices. Having a face to face conversation can as well be misinterpreted when it involves people of different genders. Social skills can be learned, and each set has a set of social skills. You cannot transfer some social skills from one environment to a different one.

Social skills affect the way we relate with others. In other words, if you are shy, you might develop some problems with the way you connect with your fellow colleges. In most cases, shyness is translated as a lack of courage and interpreted as fear. However, one can improve in such skills and lead a better life. If you are a conservative, you might have issues with development. In other words, if you are resistant to change, you might find it difficult to associate with people who are change-oriented. Thus, as an individual, you need to understand that some of these social skills that people develop affect the way they relate with each other.

It is worth noting that poor social skills can be a source of mental illness. As pointed out, social skills allow one to communicate with others effectively. Thus, if you have developed poor social skills with time, you might have some difficulties while interacting with others. In most cases, people who have negative thoughts and poor social skills tend to be lonely and more stressful as compared to people with excellent social skills. Scholars claim that loneliness is one of the causes of mental illness among individuals. Socially needy people tend to pile up issues, and they don't communicate. However, some of these social skills can be developed and grasped with time. In other words, if you want to improve on your social skills, you can adopt some by learning or watching how other people do things. The aspect is critical in the sense that it allows people to be socially active and avoid cases where loneliness pile up in terms of stress and lack of sharing. Thus, as an individual, you need to concentrate on improving your social skills as they are helpful in life. If your environment doesn't favor you, you may consider changing it and adopt one that will increase your concentration as well as improve your experience. In other words, the environment that one dwells intends to affect the way one thinks or behaves. Thus, it is vital to check on the aspects of life that surrounds you. The art is linked to the fact that the environment affects one social skill which tends to change and individual experience as well.

Chapter 2: How to Improve Your Social Skills

In life, if you are shy and struggle in fascinating conversations, you might be having issues in your social life. However, there are some of the social skills that one can gain through learning. For instance, if you aren't a social person, start behaving like one and do it smartly. Don't allow issues such as anxiety to hold you back. However, you need to make decisions and keep talking to people, whether new or old pals. Even if you are feeling nervous, make a point of improvement in terms of social skills by joining a small party or spend more time with crowds and try striking conversations. With time, you will improve on some for the social skills you feel you are deprived of. It is worth noting that if you want to draw more attention from people, make a pint of asking open-ended questions. Such questions invite people to respond with a yes or no, and the art may open up the door for more conversations. Thus, as you start the journey gaining some social skills, encourage others to talk about themselves and ask questions that will increase their interests in the topic in question. The art allows one to feel appreciated and turn out to be a charismatic speaker, let alone a good listener.

Take a look at some of the strategies you can use to improve your social skills

Listen More Talk Less

It is worth noting that good speakers are also good listeners. In other words, if you want to be a good speaker and improve on some of your social skills, you need to be a good listener as well. The art of listening is critical in the sense that it allows one to gain some social skills that are vital in life. It is worth noting that a lot of knowledge is achieved when one is listening rather than speaking. The art of talking means that you are giving away information, while the art of listening means that you are receiving information. In other words, if you train yourself to be listening more, you will gain more power and a lot of knowledge when speaking. You will have learned a lot of details that are critical when conversing.

Also if you listen more, you won`t have time to reveal anything that you will later regret. In other words, if you speak something, you won`t have a time of recalling it back. However, if you are keen on listening, you will be in an excellent position to identify some of the informing that needs to be left behind. It is worth speaking thoughtfully and removes all the doubt rather than talking a lot and later wished that you never spoke. Also, if you listen a lot, you will be in a good position of understanding issues that have been talked about. In other words, you won`t keep repeating problems that have already been discussed, and you will maintain some originality. If you are an active listener, the chances are that you will learn some of the things that annoy people. In other words, you will quickly understand some of the critical elements that make people feel upset or feel un-appreciated. However, if you are among the lot that speaks a lot without listening to what other people say, there are chances that you will have some difficulties understanding some of the issues that cause people to feel unappreciated. You will keep speaking and lose your stature as well since people won`t know what you are talking about.

Think before you speak

A good speaker is always charismatic. Good speakers always make sense in whatever they are talking about. In most cases, they think before speaking. They will spend some time trying to analyze what they feel in their hearts. Such speakers will put themselves in the shoes of their listeners and try to figure out what the audience will feel. It is worth noting that mindful thinking before one speaks is critical in life. It allows one to open up and speak sense. Also, it will enable one to figure out the exact feeling that people have as they listen to someone. If one can think criticality before speaking, one will be in a good position of creating a pleasant environment that will allow the audience to listen more and learn more from the speech.

The art of thinking before you speak is critical in the sense that it allows one to analyze whether whatever is to be spoken is true or not. In other words, if you are quick in analyzing your speech before releasing it, you will be in a good position to weigh all the information and determine what is right and what is annoying to the public. For instance, if someone asks you a question, there are chances that they might be having a clue of what is right? In most cases, if you didn't speak the truth, they will know in the long run. Thus, if you are telling a story, it is good to think whether whatever you are speaking is true or not. Don`t exaggerate issues but speak all that is real and be honest with all that has happened. The aspect is critical in the sense that it allows one to be free and avoid being in chaos when the truth is revealed. It is worth noting that it is better to stay silent rather than say something that is not helpful. It is good to consider whether whatever you comment is useful or inspiring. If whatever you are about to speak may hurt someone, it is better to remain silent and avoid annoying others. For instance, if you are about to compliment someone about the things that they have done, make a point of choosing your words to avoid hurting others. It is good to issue a congratulation message rather than praise someone at the expense of others. Also, if you are watching someone struggle with something, make a point of helping them overcome the issue silently rather than mocking them.

Mindfulness and Listening techniques

Mindfulness refers to the practice of paying attention to the present moment without making any judgments. In other words, it is the act of considering the emotional reactions that one may have over specific issues. The art of listening mindfully is critical in the sense that it allows one to be considerate of what they speak. Also, mindful listening is crucial in the sense that it will enable one to avoid a lot of distractions when listening. It is worth noting that one keenly listens and remembers only 25 % of minutes after listening to someone. In other words, if you are not careful with what you are looking, you may end up learning to note, and in the long run, you may end up being a lousy speaker as well. Listening is vital in building some of the tips that are necessary for one to be essential in life.

Mindful listening is critical in the sense that it allows one to develop some self-awareness tips that are critical in life. If you listen with your minds tuned to the speaker, you will be conscious of the environment that is surrounding you. You will also have chances of uncovering some of the unknown biases that can only be identified in listening to someone. Also, if you want to increase your empathy, make a point of being a mindful listener. In other words, you will be in a position of understanding the other person well and share their feeling.

Mindful listening is essential. It allows one to develop some of the social skills that are vital in life. If you want to practice mindful listening, you need to halt all whatever you have been doing and offer all your attention to whatever is being spoken. Also, it is good to enjoy whatever you are listening too. The aspect is critical in the sense that it allows one to create a safe environment for learning. In other words, try to create an enabling environment where you can effectively listen. It is worth noting that active listening starts from the minds. In other words, you need to alter your mindset and focus on the speaker to trap all that is being communicated. It is worth noting that active listening requires one to maintain eye contact with the speaker. You need to reflect on what you are listening to and choose to select what is vital. In other words, you need to ask yourself whether you are looking carefully or whether you are making assumptions over what is being spoken. You need to be attentive and try to make discoveries as you search. In other listen attentively and note some of the issues that are different and might be surprised that you know very little of the problems you thought you had captured in other sessions. Avoid making judgments as you listen. However, you can make conclusions or reflect on what you have heard later.

Relaxation Techniques

It is worth noting that our minds aren't robots or machines. It reaches a time where one is required to relax and allow the thoughts to regain energy. In other words, if you allow your thoughts to rest and freshens up, you will be able to capture more issues afterward. Thus, after listening and capturing new aspects of life, you need to relax and allow your minds to regain some energy. Some of the vital relaxation techniques include yoga, breath focus, mindful meditations, repetitive prayer, as well as body scan, among others. It is worth noting that conscious thinking uses a lot of energy. Therefore, one needs to relax and empty their minds, as well. For instance, the art of breath focus allows one to take slow but deep breaths that allows the thoughts to relax and focus on breathing rather than any other aspect of life. Yoga is also vital in the sense that it will enable one to empty their minds and allows them to refresh up. Such techniques are critical in the sense that one can relax and create some space for more aspects.

The Environment and your Mindfulness

A conducive environment allows one to think well and relax. In other words, if you are in a noisy environment, there are chances that you won`t be able to think right, and your mind has an issue with the art of listening as well. It is worth noting if you can`t hear well, there are chances that you won`t be able to think as well. Thus, you need to be sensitive to the environment that might affect the way you think or act.

It is worth noting that the minds of an individual are at times affected by what one does or sees. In other words, the things you see might negatively or positively affect what you see. According to the principles of colors, the hues, or the coloring around your home may have an impact on your mood as well. For instance, red symbolizes passion, and it is very vital in boosting one`s energy. On the other hand, blue and grey promote some sense of relaxation as well as tranquility. The colors can also be used as alternatives in high traffic areas. Thus, it is wise to consider the colors that surround you. It is worth noting that white is a classic home paint that exudes calmness as well as purity. However, white colors make a room to appear small or poorly lit. Yellow and green colors, on the other hand, may signify creativity or prosperity in the way. The art is linked to the fact that the colors have a perfect accent that is associated with a natural spackle as well as success.

Nature touches the minds of a person. It is worth noting that the green color is associated with the art of being mindful. The connection between life and awareness depends on the environment that one is in. In other words, if you want to concentrate and achieve a particular aspect, make a point of investing in the environment that surrounds you. In most cases, a situation with plants tends to be livelier. Lighting in a study room shows that one is the focus and ready to face reality as well. It is critical to note that your environment can be a source of stress. In other words, the way you arrange your house may affect what you think as well as the way you deliberate in issues. Consider your furnishing as well as the timber that put on your environment. The art is due to the fact that that timber, stone as well as textiles that are crafted naturally tend to be healthier and more potent than the human-made counterpart. Thus, make a point of considering some of the furniture you use in your room. Your room needs to be shining so as you can think well and act appropriately.

The effect of climate change on what human being things act or behave ought to be considered. In other words, the physical environment tends to affect the global as well as the economic disruption that one poses. The art of change in the situation tends to increase the number of people or issues in a certain. The art of being mindful depends on the factors that surround an individual. It is worth noting that most people didn't think about the things the routine things such as throwing trash in a bin or taking a shower. However, most of us are concerned with the things that promote environmental sustainability. In other words, mindfulness allows individuals to disengage from automatic thoughts and become more open to behavioral change as well as make critical choices that are helpful.

An enabling environment also supports mindful meditation. In other words, if you are in a conducive environment, you will be in a position to think right and faster than being in a noisy environment. Although there are people who tend to adopt new ways of doing things in a noisy environment, their concentrations tend to be relatively low. Practical mindfulness requires one to be attentive to all the sounds that pass across one ear. It is worth noting that being mindful doesn't involve the sensitization of the people in a particular environment. However, it consists of the art of sustaining a clean environment that allows one to think the right way. The nature that surrounds a place plays a critical role in dictating what someone thinks. In other words, the minds are strongly connected to the fundamental issues that surround it. The art of being active, happy as well as being friendly, depends on the natural features that cover a particular phenomenon. Thus, people tend to prefer places that favor them in terms of being mindful and productive. In most cases, the art of being mindful tends to improve with the environment, and a highly esteemed environment tends to offer more satisfactions hence more preferred.

Chapter3: Using Emotional Quotient to Your Advantage

What is emotional quotient?

You've probably heard of IQ (measure cognitive abilities) and not EQ. Emotional quotient is sometimes referred to as Emotional intelligence. But you might be wondering what it means. Well, this is the level of measure of personal emotional intelligence.

Also, it's the ability of a person to know their emotions and those of others and differentiate the variety of emotions correctly. Emotional quotient is useful in our day to day activities; with it, you will be able to guide your behaviors and influence that of others. After all, you can give others the power that you only possess.

Additionally, this is a vital factor in all aspects of your

life. That is your mental, spiritual, and social life. It helps you connect at a deeper self. And mold you into a desirable human being. EQ is what enables have to have serious conversations with your partner or empathize with your friend when they are going through a challenging situation or discipline your children when they do wrong.

EQ assists in emotional and social learning in children. College students with EQ get to perform better engage in more social interactions and develop constructive behaviors rather than the destructive.

Components of emotional quotient

- **Self-regulation**- You need to recognize yourself and your behaviors. Then, you regulate, express and manage your emotions
- **Self- awareness-** self-awareness acts as a foundation EQ .understanding your feelings is vital as tend to extend those emotions to others
- **Social skills** – social skills helps to foster interaction amongst people. Those with high

EQ, can interact well with others and expressing themselves is never a hard task

- **Empathy**- empathy enables you to register people feelings, known how they feel
- **Motivation-** people with high emotion quotient are self-motivated. They are happy achieving internal success, rather than external. They work hard towards their goals. Achievements such as wealth, respect, or fame don't fascinate them much. But reaching their goals is what entices them.

Characteristics of people with high EQ

1. They have a healthy work-life balance- they know how to interact with people at workplaces and air out their views when they don't agree with issues.
2. Easy going- you can talk to them, with feeling intimidated
3. They are grateful- they don't take their lives for granted, and little things fascinate them. They are thankful for everything life family, life, and also their jobs.

4. open-minded- they are not confined to their beliefs of a certain thing, but are open to new ideas and are ready to embrace them
5. They know their strengths are always willing to work on their weaknesses.
6. Forgive others easily- they don't hold grudges but forgive others
7. Know them- they know their likes, dislikes, and what they stand for in life.
8. Empathetic- they put themselves in people's shoes and can sympathize with them.

Those without emotional quotient

People are different, and forcing other people to behave in a certain way can end up bad. You don't force someone to become what you want, but you let them willingly become. EQ is not necessarily inherited but is a skill that can be developed over some time if you train.

The following are characteristics of people without EQ;

1. Unable to control their emotions. Can react veraciously to anger situations.
2. They don't care about o0her people's feelings. Or instead, they are clueless. They don't notice if someone is sad or happy.
3. They don't know how to deal with sadness or grief. In short, emotional scenes in movies don't move them. You neither cry and feel the part

Importance of developing emotional quotient

When you develop this skill you get to;

Improve your relationships. It could be with your partner's friends, neighbors, or relatives. You build on your communication skills and know-how to persuade, being open, and channel your emotions.

Understand yourself and others well- you don't forever become clueless, but you can study how you react to your emotions and also you know how others in your environment

You connect with others. Most human beings crave connection. You connect with others at a deeper level. When you connect with others; you boost your overall performance in school, home, and also work.

Skills that will assist you in developing emotional quotient

Channel your emotions well

Are you the type to break things when angry? Recognize how you react to situations. Anger can be destructive, and you should learn how to control it. Share the joyful moments with the people around you.

Learn how to motivate yourself

Appreciate yourself in everything g you do. Believe you can do anything and you will. Do something even you don't feel like doing. It could be waking up, writing, etc. self- motivation pushes you to be a better you.

Practice self- awareness

Know yourself. Investigate yourself and learn the little aspects you didn't S know about yourself. What you feel. Remove distractions from your life and learn how to motivate yourself.

Recognize the way other people feel.

Understand people and listen to people more. People are vulnerable. When you recognize other people's feelings, you will be able to foster a romantic atmosphere, also respect other people's needs and wants. You become selfless.

Self-awareness techniques

Self-awareness means that you can recognize yourself on a personal level. This is s inclusive of your strengths weaknesses, emotions, thoughts, and also believes. Self-awareness makes you understand people and return their feelings,

Also, you can correct your behaviors and improve yourself for the better things about you start to change, and you become more optimistic when it comes to life. Self-awareness increases your level of EQ and gives you a sense of direction in your future. Lastly, you learn how to optimize yourself.

The following are self-awareness techniques:

Have a journal

In this journal scribble everything and anything that goes on in your life. Your, goals, your, strengths, your weakness, your success stories, among other things, a journal helps you free yourself from various emotions, especially those of anger. You vent out and in return, become happier.

You learn to appreciate yourself more and work hard towards achieving your goals

Be objective about yourself.

Self-awareness enable3 you learn and accept yourself the way you are. You learn more things about yourself. What perceptions do you have when you experience certain aspects of life?

Learn how you react to happy situations, sad situations, or people. Write things you are proud of and what makes you. Being objective enables you to encourage others to be the better versions of them, as you are.

Meditate

Meditation is a good, mindfulness activity. It helps you relax your mind. This is a high daily activity of self-awareness.

Find a quiet, comfortable place to start your meditation. Then, close your eyes and be in the moment and, lastly breathe. Meditation helps you relax. You reflect on yourself, your goals, and assist you to focus more.

Ask feedback from your friends.

Feedback is important. Ask your friends for honest feedback. They should tell you how you behave and how they perceive you. They act as a mirror. Honest feedback will enable you to know yourself more and also know the qualities to improve.

Interrogate yourself.

Ask yourself questions concerning a different aspect of your life.

They could be your likes, dislikes, what you are good at, things that make you happy or the one that interests, write down on your journal. You can always review later.

Take personality tests

Several personality tests are online. With them, you are enabled to measure your innate capabilities as a human being. The test gives you a good self-awareness ground, and you can improve. Personality tests don't need to be 100%.

Finally, Self-awareness is crucial as it helps you become the best version of yourself.

Self -management

Self-management means taking responsibilities and the actions that you take in life. You become the boss of you and regulate your behaviors, emotions, thoughts, in different situations.

The following are rules of self-management rules. They are what guide you in your self-management journey:

- **Cultivate trust**- you need to created trust or be trustworthy so that people will have faith in you.
- **Be yourself -** don't copy others. You are amazing the way that you are. Copying others will stop you from living your best life. Be original
- **Have a courtesy** -courteous phrases like thank you, sorry, and excuse me don't cost any dime.

They make you responsible, and a respected person as you mind what others feel.

- **Always learn to say no-** you don't have to say yes, to all situations. Saying no to friends outing is okay as it can give you more time for yourself.

- **Speak up-** don't be quiet when things are wrong; people need to know you and what you stand for. You don't expect people to hear what is in your heart or mind, dear.

- **Keep your promises.** When you promise a thing to someone strive to fulfill it.   Keeping promises enhances the trust that people have in you

- **Take care of yourself-** If you don't, then who will?   Make yourself the priority. Exercise, meditate, ad eats healthily and have fun in all things that fascinate you.

Key self-management skills

The following skills will help you manage your skills.

Initiative

From the name, this means that you take actions concerning different events that take place in your life. You don't need one to tell you that something needs to be done but, instead you, do it. You are not pushed but you self-motivate yourself.

Organization

With organization skills that plan what you need from most relevant to the least important. The organization ensures you get most done out of your daily activities.

Accountability

Accountability means that you are responsible for yourself. When things go wrong, you can rectify without blaming others. Blaming sucks and it's only for those who don't want to own up to their mistakes . Accountability enables you to improve your skills.

Importance of self- management

Self- management enables you to take advantage of rare opportunities.

When called upon to take on duty, you don't hesitate since you know how to organize yourself and are ready to grasp any opportunities that present themselves.

Focus on your goals-

For goals to achieved, several things need to take place. That is lots of work hard and commitment. But, self-management becomes your drive to do anything.

Become comfortable when working and know how to organize time

The saying goes to say that time is money. When you know how to plan your time, then you get a lot done in your life. You become happier as your productivity rates improve. When working, you don't have any worries because you know yourself more.

Control your emotions

Knowing how to deal with situations and finally you know to behave. Getting along with others won't be difficult, as you have empathetic s skills in you. You know what you want and exactly what you stand for.

Social awareness

Social awareness is the understanding of one's environment or community. That could be the culture, norms and regulations, and problems. You understand your environmental well and discover how to deal with the conditions surrounding it. Also, you can interact with people and know how they feel. With this, you can deal with intrapersonal and societal problems.

With this, you can solve personal problems. In this technological world, Social media and video conferencing is not a big deal. But in reality, people crave attention. Technology has resulted in social isolation.

Importance of social awareness

When you lack social awareness, then, you will be a misfit to society. You need to understand what is going on around your environment. The advantages include:

- It helps to understand and communicate with people. Speaking to people is important. When you as aware of what is going around you, then you will be able to conduct a conversation.
- You become more empathetic- social awareness enables you to notice pain in people. Hence, you help others deal with their grief.
- You develop problem-solving skills- when a problem arises, then you can come up with a solution and solve it.
- You get respect from people- people begin respecting you as they feel you understand them and can solve certain situations.

How to develop social -awareness skills

Become self-aware

When you know who you are, then you know exactly who you are. You observe and react to the situations of others who need your help. You think of others and help them deal with different situations in their life.

Practice forgiveness

Holding grudges is not good for yourself or even others. It creates hostility. Forgiveness improves the quality of your life. You became aware of other people's feelings. Lastly, you deal with people in a better way.

Be mindful

Whatever you do, your actions and feelings, you need to be aware of people living around you. Be polite and calm. This will connect with people more and enhance your happiness

Affirm regularly

Every morning in the mirror, tell yourself that you are an important person and you are able. Affirmation improves yourself self- awareness. You even start appreciating those in your environment more.

Listen more, talk less

People love being listened to. Let people rant about their problem to you, and you can offer them solutions. Or rather a shoulder to lean on

Think before you act

You need to be fully aware before speaking or answering a question. Some answers can be offending, so always try to be careful.

Make yourself better

Every day you should be competing with yourself. You ought to strive to be a better person than you were yesterday. So each minute tries to better yourself. The following are some ways to achieve this:

Go offline

Try it for a month, and you wouldn't regret it. Social media has a lot of noise. Being offline will not only help you love yourself but also appreciate you more?

Observe

The world has numerous opportunities. It awaits people to take advantage of such situations. Learn from the mistake, choose wisdom from the words of people you admire, come up with ideas from your evening walk. You just need to do is open your eyes and see.

Read

Read a lot. Books, newspapers, magazines, and blogs. There is lots of information on your books which helps you improve yourself. The best part is you can choose any genre you want. Do you love technology, health, or travel then go for it. With time your knowledge of things will improve.

Stop procrastination

This is a killer of dreams. Just rise from that comfy situation and dare to become. Do you doubt yourself? You can.

Help others

You wouldn't know how this will make other people smile. Small acts like helping an older man to cross the road, or opening a door for someone is not only fulfilling to you but also the other person.

Surprise people

It could be you, workmate, friend, or parent. Make a smile on people's faces. They need it. People will love you and appreciate you more.

Writing

Write about anything. It could be to create your day, a person you admire and adore. Writing helps you cultivate discipline. You'll want to practice your skill daily.

Compliment yourself.

You are beautiful and smart. Compliment yourself every day and congratulate yourself on the little achievements that you make.

Practical examples

Emotional intelligent takes a massive part in our daily activities and your workplace.

How people conduct themselves in a meeting

Meeting where everyone talks and they aren't listening to each other can be chaotic. Hence, reflecting people's ego. But, when one person speaks at a time, then, evidently, people are listening to each other. EQ is at plays a role in this. It just shows how people have respect and care about the other party's emotions.

People expressing themselves in an office

When people can express themselves openly, without being hindered is a practical example of EQ. This depicts their feelings, views, and opinions is important to the organization. The exchanges should be in a respectful manner.

Organizations, where the employees are free to speak out, are pleasant. When search issues are rated out, an emotionally intelligent boss wouldn't be offended bit would instead take affirmative action and congratulate the person for being free.

Flexibility

Emotionally intelligent people have a warm heart. They know that they work with human beings and nit machines. They would instill strict rules on the work environment. Instead, they understand that people are different and respect their work as long as the job is done.

Freedom and space to be creative

Organizations should create room for creativity. Refusing people the idea is not only unethical but also terrible. When a superior suppresses one thought, then it can only show that their emotional quotient is low.

There is compassion

Arguments, in homes, workplaces usually occur. Dealing with people's mood swings, changed attitude says a lot about your EQ level. Being able to understand that a person's mood is terrible, and responding to the other person calmly is equally important when an employee fails to do their work well, then, the leader should think before scolding him and throwing hurtful words to them. They should motivate them and encourage them to work hard. The result will enhance teamwork.

Interacting out of work hours

Interacting during lunch breaks, chatting on the corridors, catching a bus after work shows social behavior. Social activities ensure that people have funned, share their joyful moments, and also their sorrowful moments. Thus, they bond. This depicts how emotionally intelligent they are, and connect with other people and create social interactions.

Developing emotional quotient personally

When you are upset or angry, and you show it on yourself, then this will likely push people away from you. Learning how to control your emotions would make you friendlier.

You need to have self-awareness and self-cautious be to achieve this. Then use self- regulation to develop emotional quotient. Learning to calm is important since it doesn't influence our decision-making process.

Chapter 4: How to Reduce Stress and Anxiety

Mindfulness

What do we mean when we look at the term mindfulness. Mindfulness is looked at as an art. This is something that people can practice from time to time. Mindfulness then is the art of focusing on a particular activity so that at the end of it all they can become better at the activity. This is done by all groups of people whether the working class, students and other people. It is used to enhance concentration at the activities one is focusing on. It increases the performance of the activity.

So after knowing all about what mindfulness entails, it is important to know how to increase it. The first thing is by meditating once you wake up in the morning. I know how you are wondering how that is even impossible. This helps one to reflect on what goals they expect to achieve at the end of the day. Once one knows what the want it is easy to concentrate in order to get it easily. The daily morning meditation is soothing and it helps you to look forward to the expected. Thus helps in building mindfulness in a particular person.

The next thing is one should take a break. This is what people call taking time out. This helps one clear their mind. It is not easy to concentrate when you are really tired. When one is tired they brain shuts off since it cannot take any more of the information or tasks that one is giving it. One should rest preferably sleep, taking a hobby or watching television. These are great ways to distract oneself and recollect themselves. It is important that one should be well-rested if they want to achieve maximum mindfulness in one's life.

Another thing is that one should bring together all his or her thoughts. One should ensure that is thinking singly and not in multiple directions one should ensure that they are able to bring their thoughts together. One cannot focus on anything if their head is everywhere. One should keep their head in one place and avoid any distractions. Find a way to put your thoughts in a composed manner. It maybe is through exercise, meditation, and other methods too. Putting one's thoughts together is very important at any time. This is another great way to improve one's mindfulness.

Also, there is another way that is eating well. Eating well means eating healthy and filling oneself until one is full. One can never work if he or she is hungry. Also eating healthy counts since it allows someone to be strong and immune to diseases. If one is sick then they cannot concentrate on anything that they do. These small facts make eating well very essential. The body and the mind are connected hence eating and mindfulness go hand in hand. So it is important to follow an eating schedule if you really want to improve on your daily mindfulness.

Lastly, there is knowing and understanding others' mindfulness. Before you fully understand yourself then you must understand others fully. It may be how they think or work it depends on you. One cannot work alone others count for your success. It is great to know others live their lives if you want to blend in with them. One cannot just be an island interaction is very important. If one is comfortable with other people it makes it easy to concentrate on other things. The fear of others may hinder one's concentration and thus may cause one's mindfulness to be very low.

Mindfulness is important in our daily lives and we should maintain it as always. One should work on improving their level of mindfulness for better results.

Social Anxiety

Before I dwell on what is social anxiety, I will first give out the meaning of anxiety. Anxiety, therefore, is the fear that one gets of a certain activity or occurrence. So what then is social anxiety? Social anxiety is then the fear of interacting with other people in society. It basically forms the name of this type of anxiety. It is also called social phobia. Phobia is the other name for fear.

There are so many causes of social anxiety am going to mention a few to make you understand how this type of anxiety comes about. The first cause is that it may emerge from abuse. That may be from emotional, physical and sexual abuse. It may not matter at what age it happens but if at all one goes through abuse they tend to shut off the world. They also live in fear of other people this makes them avoid them, in the long run, they become loners. They are mostly alone and sad for most of their time.

Another cause is that one might have undergone bullying or is undergoing bullying. This is mostly done to someone by people who are of the same age as the victim. This affects the person physically, mentally and psychologically. That means one is affected very largely. This makes one take a step at ignoring others due to the fear they might have. Bullying scars one for life and that is very painful. Their coping mechanism is just to avoid other people. These people have to go through therapy if they are going to recover. This is a cause that mainly affects students.

Also, there is the fact that one could have lost a parent or someone close to them. This is the hardest thing one can undergo. It affects one in so many ways. One's emotions are usually all over the place. One tends to go into a metaphorical dark corner. They do not understand what they are feeling or really going through. It is usually rough and may decide to push people away. They think that they will be better off alone than with others by his or her side. This is one of the major causes of social phobia.

Another thing that is a very good cause is conflicts or violence in the family. When someone is in a family that is well not thriving in a harmonious way then they tend to keep their distance from people. Since one spends most of their time as a kid with their family they tend to believe people are like their family in terms of their behavior. If one's family is violent and unstable then that is what they will passive for the whole world. This then leads them to keep away from others due to the fear that they have.

The last cause is the reaction a woman gets after giving birth. Women have different reactions once they give birth. This is because they are very different. Some women are happy and accept themselves easily for who they have become. This also includes the body changes after birth. There is also another group of women who really respond negatively after giving birth. They hate their bodies and find it hard to accept themselves. They then avoid people since they are ashamed of being body-slammed about how their bodies are not perfect anymore. This makes a major cause for the current generation.

Social anxiety happens every day. It happens to most people and they usually do not know how to handle this kind of anxiety. The main thing that the victims should use therapy. They should use psychological therapy to their advantage for them to become very normal like the other people.

Reprogram Your Mindset

People often ask themselves what mindset really is. The mindset of a person is how one takes certain information or activity either positively or negatively in the mind. What someone thinks is very important. Whether someone thinks positively or negatively about something makes the total difference. They are the ones that determine your success or failures in a particular thing. They are very important aspects that most people tend to ignore not knowing how much they influence their lives. They are also inbuilt but can be easily changed but by the person himself.

The first thing one has to do is leave what they are used to. This like the comfort place of someone. One should be open to trying new things in their life. One should not be afraid of taking a really huge step. One should be a very huge risker in life. Always take things like taking water. That means taking a positive step to a new thing and then see what comes next. The more you dive into new things in a positive manner the better the results that come out at the very end. This is a very important step to take.

The other thing is finding people who are just like you. That means finding people who have the same mindset as you. That means people who share your goals and aspirations. They are people who view life like you do and enjoy it as you do too. They act like the object that pushes you to try new things. They give you advice and also stick by your side no matter what may pop up. Their perspective on life is quite similar to yours so clashing of yours and their opinions are nearly impossible.

Also, one should note the situation they are in and see what mindset they should take in after some thought. This may seem absurd but all situations have different responses. That flatly means that even the mindset put in should different too, they cannot share the same mindsets of the person. These differences give someone a challenge and at the end of the day, one gets a ton of exercise in matters of the mindset. One has to know what mindset to apply and whether it is suitable or not. This helps someone to know their way through life and everything it brings.

Another thing to do is to change one's habits to fit one's new mindset. It is only fair that once one thinks of changing they should be ready to make a full-on change. This is actually a big step that one has to take for easy moving on. This allows someone to change their ideas and how they execute them. In the very end, one becomes a new person. That is a new mindset and new behavior. This should be adopted if you really want to maintain their newly attained mindset then this is very important.

It is good to know that mindset is the thing that allows you to be confident and do new things. When one has a great mindset then their confidence is great too. That means one can do anything and they can achieve anything. It also makes some to trust themselves through everything. One can try things they thought they could never do but it all depends on the mindset. This is a great topic to look at. There is more to mindset and how it works in human beings but am only giving the few tips that are above.

Practice Assertiveness

Assertiveness is the art of someone standing with their decision no matter what. This is about believing in yourself regardless of the situation. One is supposed to stick by themselves and not change even if the pressure exerted at the time is very immense it does not matter.

There are so many ways to increase your assertiveness. I am going to discuss a few to act as a guide for you to use. The first way is by not allowing one to sway your opinions. Many people call it agreeing to the disagreeing concept. This is when you and others are discussing and end up one-two different sides then it is important to listen to their side but not join him or her in their opinion. One should be cautious of what they want and not let others change what they know and believe in their ideas.

The next thing is being a good listener. Even if though am saying one should not be swayed it is important to listen to the others. The opinions of others matter at all times. All you have to do is sit and listen to their ideas and before you know it he or she will be listening to you. It is two-way traffic for this situation. The idea is to understand the concept the person is looking at and he or she should do the same. This, in the end, leaves one knowing themselves and the others too.

The last thing is to avoid being guilty. Guilt can lead you to not do what you really want. Guilt can make one forget about their own decisions. This is then should be something one can easily avoid after all. One should be proud of what they decide and should feel. One should know that their opinions are valid and right. One cannot just please everyone and if you could you would be miserable at the very end. The more one understands this concept then the more it becomes easy to be assertive. This is very important in the process of being assertive.

All the above aspects show how one can be more social with others. Socializing is not that hard but we learn new things every day. These new things help one to deal with new people in their lives. It is great to know how to deal with people every time. The more you read the more you see how social skills are easy. All the aspects work differently. That means they all work separately. The mindset, assertiveness, and others work towards improving people to people skills.

This is very elaborate and the mentioned aspects are just but a few.

Chapter 5: Emotional Intelligence

What is Emotional Intelligence?

To understand emotional intelligence then one must understand the term emotions. So what are these so-called emotions? Emotions are the behavior one shows after a certain event. They are many including happiness, sadness, mad or angry and others. They are all designed for different occasions and they are strictly used where required. Emotional intelligence comes in here. Emotional intelligence hence is the ability of one to decipher and understand their emotions this also includes where and how to use one's own emotions. If one is able to do this he or she has emotional intelligence.

To understand more of emotional intelligence then one should look at the components of emotional intelligence. I am only going to mention and discuss five of these components. This is what makes the background of emotional intelligence.

The first is knowing oneself. This is known as self-awareness. This helps one to understand their emotions. You cannot understand others' emotions without understanding yours. It is important to see the graph or patterns of how you react to different situations. It is important to master your moods without criticizing yourself. Get to learn who you are and appreciate it. Then after you have done this reading others and knowing how to respond to them is well pretty much easy. This helps someone work on controlling their emotions at all times. It also helps one to know how to direct one's emotions after all.

The other component is being able to keep oneself in check. This is often known as self-regulation. This is where one has to train himself or herself in the art of keeping their emotions in check. This works hand in hand with self-awareness. Once you know how your emotions work then it is easy to keep them in check. How to do that all depends on you. It is one's responsibility to know and to keep their emotions in check. Others cannot that for you hence it is you who has the power when it comes to emotions.

Also, there is motivation as a component. This is where one has to have an interest in learning and improving themselves. In this topic, the learning and the improving involve the emotional part. One should be ready to learn about his or her emotions and to know how to improve them at the very end. One should be enthusiastic about what all their emotions are like. One should be able to accept themselves at the very end. It is always advisable to be motivated to know themselves even better than they think they know them. This step is important as the rest.

The next is being able to put yourself in other's shoes especially if they are in trouble or at a hard place. This feeling and virtue are known as empathy. Most people confuse empathy and sympathy. Sympathy is feeling pity for someone who is not faring well. These two meanings show the difference between these two terms. They are interrelated but are totally different. Empathy is a virtue that when expressed shows that someone can feel. That means that the person can be able to express their emotions and that is a good sign. It shows a sign of humanity.

Lastly, there are social skills. These refer to how people interact with others. Emotions usually hold a big place in terms of interacting with others. When one has not put their emotions in check then it is easy for them to blow out when they are communicating with other people thus ruining their social life all in all. When one has their emotions in check on the other hand then it will be easy to communicate with others without pissing them off. It is important to remember that their feelings and other feelings are to be considered always.

It is good to note that all the components are the key to emotions and daily living. Emotions help one to socialize with others. They are the root of humanity. They all work together and differently all together: the components. It is all-important to know that your emotions and others too are important. The components work to making one a better person emotionally. If one becomes better emotionally then they are bound to be better in their aspects too and that also makes someone a better person at the very end of it all and makes you better with people.

How to use your emotional quotient to understand your needs

Emotional intelligence is also known as emotional quotient. This is looking and being able to read one's emotions in the long run of things. One should be able to use his or her emotions in the right manner without worrying. Also, there is the ability to keep things in check. This is keeping one's emotions in balance especially when one is conversing with others.

The following are ways in which we can use our emotional quotient. The first is used is that one understands more of others than oneself. We have seen that emotions do not only revolve on oneself but affect everyone that is around you. The more you look at it the easy the concept is. It is all about socializing which happens every day. Since one is in constant interaction with others it is important to understand them that means in the emotional side in this context. Since one is focused on make themselves emotional fitting for others they focus on what others want from him or her.

It helps one to get into more of very personal communication. Emotions make some so human. There are feelings of empathy and sympathy which are so touchy and personal. They help someone to get into the groove of living with others. Emotions make you care about others and that makes you vulnerable. It also helps someone to be able to share his or her feelings with others. One becomes more open to people's help and also their opinions. One is able to get the treatment they give to others given to them at any time.

The other one is being able to talk and inquire about others and what they might be feeling this is very important. It is interconnected with the issue of personal communication. With this one is supposed to involve themselves with others' lives if this going to work. This is usually possible when people know each other and are open at saying anything to each other. Trust is formed at this point or stage of life. It is good to always inquire about others it helps to show care or concern. This is another perfect use of emotional intelligence.

The other point to know is what people want out of you or your deeds. This is what is called expectations. Since one becomes less self-centered and more of what others want, one becomes more observing and thus one can know what others want. With that knowledge one is able to know how to emotionally act in that particular situation. One knows how to fulfill others' expectations once one knows what they are like. This is a great step taken after one becomes more of a people person and also after one decides to have very personal relationships and conversations with others.

Also, the other use is the ability to increase one's attention. This is the ability of one to focus on the current situation and that is in an emotional way. This is where someone listens and focuses on themselves and others all together. It is easy to see things in their light when the attention is full. This point helps one to focus on oneself and all others. One may indulge in anything and should make sure it gets to be okay.

This should be important it helps one to deal with others in a great way since you give them your time.

The other thing is to increase the ability of someone to feel what others are feeling. This is putting yourself in other's shoes. It is usually a way to show support to others and their problems or even issues. It shows that one cares and is concerned about others and that makes one seem so nice. This gesture shows maturity in one's emotions and life. It is also a very great use of the emotions one has. One gets connected to others through this feeling of empathy. It works for those people who are sympathetic too since they are interrelated.

The last one is that one should put their needs far and let others need ahead. One should be less self-centered and care about others. One should be considerate of others. This is the basic rule of emotions. They might be yours but they are made to deal with others for them to work efficiently. They are meant to make you feel more of what human one can be. They make you a better person at the time you understand them. Your needs should become after others. Make others your priority and see who you become at the end.

The following shows the uses of emotional intelligence. The help one get through daily life and all its challenges and what's more without somehow one becomes a little lost. Every day one should work on their emotions even if it may seem absurd. They are basics to live at all times. It is important that one tends on their emotions. They are like gardens which when planed one has to tendon them at all times. Emotions are very key in life they work with the body and mind side by side and for that, they should be respected.

The emotional intelligence scale

The emotional intelligence scale was developed in 1998 by a man named Schutte. It was based on the reflective of dimensions model which was formed in 1990. It was a scale that had 33 things or ideas in it. They included knowing when one could speak of their issues, how to face the issues that come with life and also trying things with a new and bright positivity that burns in each person.

There were four questions and tests that were brought to light afterward. This was: the first was the emotional quotient inventory 2.0. this test has empirical evidence meaning it is accepted worldwide as a valid scientific test. It has been developed slowly by global research. It is delivered online thus suitable for this century. It is used for people the ages 16 and above. The test itself has open-ended questions and look at one's life. It also takes a maximum of 30 minutes to be complete. It looks at matters of particular skills and also the issue of conflict resolution. The results are bent to find the emotions of a person and also how they help one in making decisions. That means it looks at the daily performance of someone at their basic social institutions. Since they are online after the test is taken the results are processed online and are immediately sent online too. They also look at the five components that affect the emotional intelligence of a person. The test is a free procedure. The person administering the test should be qualified for such a task. That may require people like a psychiatrist or other related professionals in that field.

The second one is called the profile of emotional competence. Its results do not combine inter-personal and intra-personal emotional intelligence. It looks at the components of emotional intelligence. This test takes time and a lot of research to validate but it is as free as can be. It consists of 50 items and takes up to 15 minutes to administer. It also has a short form where there are just 20 items and the time for taking it is 10 minutes in the max. it must be administered by a psychologist who has specialized in emotional intelligence and all. It is available for clinical research.

The third question is known as the trait emotional intelligence questionnaire. It is free of charge and is on academic and clinical trials. It has both the full form and the short form. The full form has 153 items that have distinctive facets and a global trait too. The short-form as from the name has 30 items and is used to measure the global trait. This comes from the full form. The name of this test uses questionnaires to find out the emotional intelligence of people that take the following test. In the questionnaire, there are gathering ratings that are represented. There are both 360 degrees. They are mainly used by children who are 8 to 12 years of age. They are the most suitable for this kind of emotional test and are very age-appropriate. This is because there is a questionnaire made just for the children. For this kind of questionnaire, it contains 75 items and has a 5 point scale. It also looks into some facets of children. This is very friendly for all ages since their questionnaires are there for everyone and for all the ages that are there.

The last question is Wong's emotional intelligence scale (WEIS). It is a self-report measure of emotional intelligence. It works with four dimensions of ability. They are divided into two parts. The first 20 parts one gets to choose their reflective reactions and the other part is made up of the 20 ability pairs. The questions used here are similar to those used in emotional intelligence tests. They look at one's strengths and weaknesses and also looks at one's personality at large. It checks on issues such as the emotions that arise in one. The other is to know and understand how one can respond to a certain situation. Also one answers how they can bring more people into their fold. The other is to know what makes one feel happy and contented with life and what makes you feel sad and like you want to give up. Also, there is describing how you feel using your words all along. There is also understanding how others feel in a given situation that they might be in at the time. Finally, is knowing when you are really angry and finding a solution as fast as you can.

These scales of emotional intelligence have been made to suit everyone. Each looks at emotions differently. Some look at self-report, the other-report and finally are the ability measures. Every scale has its features which I have dwelt in. they all matter if you really want to understand emotions. It may seem complex but I have tried to simplify it for the sake of everyone. This is a very good topic. It is interesting and it is something one can take up reading. Find everything that may seem unanswered about human emotions. Hope this gives a good and clear picture of things.

The measurement of emotional intelligence is just like any other test meaning there is the capability of comparison. It helps to know how high or low your emotional intelligence is. Their several questions are asked once in a while in this kind of test. What I mean is the question of emotions. There so many questions that are asked all to know emotional human behavior. There is a question on moving on. This considers if you are able to move on from an ordeal or if you get stuck and never seem to move on. This helps one to know if they are emotionally vulnerable or they are strong to accept the way things are and get a new fresh start for themselves.

There is also a question on whether one is able to know and act on their feelings. This leads to the question do you know if you are happy, sad, mad or even angry? These are some basic feelings you should be able to detect very easily and if not one should train themselves so that they become better at it. The questions are many more but those two give you a clue on which questions are asked about emotions. These questions when answered determine how well you are with your emotions. To be specific this two questions when answered yes that mean you have high emotional intelligence and when your answer is no then your emotional intelligence is very low.

Chapter 6: Emotional Intelligence Assessment

Instructions for this assessment

Emotional intelligence is an important measure of how we relate with other people, influence their lives and react to situations. The test is meant to help you gauge how much you have grown in making relationships with other people better, and realize the areas that need to be improved. The test is geared towards making you a better person, and not to make you feel bad about yourself. The questions are in form of situations that we experience in our daily lives when relating with people, especially those who are closer to us; the answers are the feedback we give to the described situations in form of how we behave feel or even think. When giving the answers, for you to get an accurate assessment of yourself, be honest. After taking the test, you will be required to calculate your score following the score scales provided. The recommendations on how to improve your emotional intelligence will be provided; use it according to your score.

Relationship management

Emotional intelligence helps one to identify emotions, understand, and manage, and use emotions to help others or yourself. EI has divided into four clusters and one of them is relationship management, which consists of seven competencies. Visionary leadership, which helps one to inspire groups and individuals; making others grow, which entails supporting other people to strengthen their abilities through listening to their feedback and guiding them appropriately. Relationship management also involves influencing other people, and the individual should be able to have a variety of strategies that considers maintaining your integrity. Influencing people entails so many things such as having clear communication and listening to the people you are managing, convincing them to take up ideas that are useful to the company or themselves. In relationship management, one should also have better strategies for dealing with conflicts that arise between those he or she is managing and amongst themselves. It involves team methods of conflict resolution, maintaining a relationship with other people and building bonds that will help in working together.

Emotional Intelligence Test for a Relationship Management

Answer the following question by selecting the best answer that applies to you

1. I always respect the view of other people during a discussion.

Agree to   ◌   ◌   ◌   ◌   ◌   Disagree

2. I always great my juniors in the morning and at the end of the day ask them about their daily activities.

Agree on   ◌   ◌   ◌   ◌   ◌   Disagree

*3. I always start to try to control emotions that control my moods.

Agree on   ◌   ◌   ◌   ◌   ◌   Disagree

4. I always make up time to talk to my friends and bond with them.

Agree on   ◌   ◌   ◌   ◌   ◌   Disagree

5. I always try to initiate the reconciliation process with my spouse or girlfriend.

Agree on   ◌   ◌   ◌   ◌   ◌   Disagree

6. I know what I am good at and what I am not.

Agree on   ◌   ◌   ◌   ◌   ◌   Disagree

7. Most of the time I find ways to relieve stress

through taking a walk in the park

Agree on   ○   ○   ○   ○   ○   Disagree

8. After doing something, I value feedback from my spouse or friend

Agree on   ○   ○   ○   ○   ○   Disagree

9. I always dress up to look good for my spouse.

Agree on   ○   ○   ○   ○   ○   Disagree

10. I always know my feeling towards a particular situation.

Agree on   ○   ○   ○   ○   ○   Disagree

11. I prefer criticizing people more than I praise them for the good things they have done.

Agree on   ○   ○   ○   ○   ○   Disagree

12. I stay fit and healthy through exercise and eating a balanced diet.

Agree on   ⊂   ⊂   ⊂   ⊂   ⊂   Disagree

13. I take some time out of my work to talk with my workmates.

Agree on   ⊂   ⊂   ⊂   ⊂   ⊂   Disagree

14. I try to keep the effects of my stress to other people as low as possible.

Agree on   ⊂   ⊂   ⊂   ⊂   ⊂   Disagree

15. I like knowing more about my partner's family and their progress.

Agree on   ⊂   ⊂   ⊂   ⊂   ⊂   Disagree

16. I know my spouse's favorite yogurt flavor and always try to know any changes.

Agree on   ⊂   ⊂   ⊂   ⊂   ⊂   Disagree

17. I always remain in control of my emotions during arguments.

Agree on   ⊂   ⊂   ⊂   ⊂   ⊂   Disagree

18. I always make a commitment and stay focused.

Agree on   ⊂   ⊂   ⊂   ⊂   ⊂   Disagree

19. I am a good financial manager at my house.

Agree on   ⊂   ⊂   ⊂   ⊂   ⊂   Disagree

20. I always speak my mind when we are having an argument with my friends

Agree on   ⊂   ⊂   ⊂   ⊂   ⊂   Disagree

21. I like being optimistic about my future.

Agree on   ◌   ◌   ◌   ◌   ◌   Disagree

22. I always arrange for a getaway party for my friends.

Agree on   ◌   ◌   ◌   ◌   ◌   Disagree

23. I always keep my priorities right.

Agree on   ◌   ◌   ◌   ◌   ◌   Disagree

24. I always seek help when I am in need.

Agree on   ◌   ◌   ◌   ◌   ◌   Disagree

25. I release tension though stretching my muscles and breathing in deeply.

Agree on   ◌   ◌   ◌   ◌   ◌   Disagree

26. I like being updated on my partner's passion, tastes, and preferences.

Agree on   ○   ○   ○   ○   ○   Disagree

27. I like multiplying money though doing business.

Agree on   ○   ○   ○   ○   ○   Disagree

28. When I realize that it is me who is on the wrong, I quickly apologize.

Agree on   ○   ○   ○   ○   ○   Disagree

29. I like encouraging my friends to achieve their dreams rather than point out their failures.

Agree on   ○   ○   ○   ○   ○   Disagree

30. I do not always take up my view; I often take time to listen to the views of others.

Agree on   ○   ○   ○   ○   ○   Disagree

31. I sometimes use humor to cool down tensions

caused by conflicts.

Agree on   ○   ○   ○   ○   ○   Disagree

32. being honest is my thing, even when the situation requires a little lie.

Agree on   ○   ○   ○   ○   ○   Disagree

33. When I am stressed I try to find out what is causing it and get rid of it.

Agree on   ○   ○   ○   ○   ○   Disagree

34. I easily talk about how I feel with my spouse.

Agree on   ○   ○   ○   ○   ○   Disagree

35. I do not like keeping one job for a long time.

Agree on   ○   ○   ○   ○   ○   Disagree

36. I regularly ask for feedback on what excites my

partner in terms of sexual pleasures

Agree on ○ ○ ○ ○ ○ Disagree

37. I watch my health and engage in activities that promote it.

Agree on ○ ○ ○ ○ ○ Disagree

38. I do not like being caught off guard; I always try to plan to deal with hard times ahead.

Agree on ○ ○ ○ ○ ● Disagree

39. I like celebrating with my partner his or her birthday and anniversaries.

Agree on ○ ○ ○ ○ ○ Disagree

40. When solving a conflict, I like all of us to be winners at the end of a resolution.

Agree on ○ ○ ○ ○ ○ Disagree

41. I do not understand the importance of money management.

Agree on   ◦   ◦   ◦   ◦   ◦   Disagree

42. I always know what excites my partner and what does not.

Agree on   ◦   ◦   ◦   ◦   ◦   Disagree

43. I do not like seeking help on sexual problems with my partner.

Agree on   ◦   ◦   ◦   ◦   ◦   Disagree

44. I always seek to know my friend's dreams and aspirations

Agree on   ◦   ◦   ◦   ◦   ◦   Disagree

45. I try to swim out of difficult situations in order to succeed.

Agree on ⊂ ⊂ ⊂ ⊂ ⊂ Disagree

46. I constantly rebuke my partner on their past mistakes.

Agree on ⊂ ⊂ ⊂ ⊂ ⊂ Disagree

47. I always take time to enjoy intimacy with my partner.

Agree on ⊂ ⊂ ⊂ ⊂ ⊂ Disagree

48. I invest more of what I earn to make my relationship with my partner better.

Agree on ⊂ ⊂ ⊂ ⊂ ⊂ Disagree

49. I always keep in touch with my workmates even when not at work.

Agree on ⊂ ⊂ ⊂ ⊂ ⊂ Disagree

50. I am always reminded about our anniversary by my partner.

Agree on   ○   ○   ○   ○   ○   Disagree

51. I have goals that I always strive to achieve.

Agree on   ○   ○   ○   ○   ○   Disagree

52. I have an insurance plan for those who depend on me.

Agree on   ○   ○   ○   ○   ○   Disagree

53. I like improving myself in terms of skills.

Agree on   ●   ○   ○   ○   ○   Disagree

54. I try to calm down my friends and comfort them when they are feeling sad.

Agree on   ⌐   ⌐   ⌐   ⌐   ⌐   Disagree

55. When things are not going well between me and my partner, I try to make things working without blame.

Agree on   ⌐   ⌐   ⌐   ⌐   ⌐   Disagree

56. I reflect on my dreams and aspirations regularly.

Agree on   ⌐   ⌐   ⌐   ⌐   ⌐   Disagree

57. I try to understand disturbing events in a positive way.

Agree on   ⌐   ⌐   ⌐   ⌐   ⌐   Disagree

*58. I find time to check on what is disturbing my friends.

Agree on   ⌐   ⌐   ⌐   ⌐   ⌐   Disagree

59. I keep my weight in check always.

Agree on   ○   ○   ○   ○   ○   Disagree

*60. I let my friends choose tasks for themselves when we are out having fun.

Agree on   ○   ○   ○   ○   ○   Disagree

61. When a friend is struggling with his or her tasks, I try to help him or her finds his or her way out.

Agree   ○   ○   ○   ○   ○   Disagree

62. I always take a break from arguments when things are not working out.

Agree on   ○   ○   ○   ○   ○   Disagree

63. During arguments, I always try not to hurt myself but do not care if my partner gets hurt or not.

Agree on   Disagree

64. I regularly look at my irrational way of doing things and try to correct them.

Agree on   Disagree

65. I always accept forgiveness from a friend who has hurt me.

Agree on   Disagree

66. I listen to my partner's problems more often and try to help him or her to solve.

Agree on   Disagree

67. I do not care about what affects my partner sexually.

Agree on   Disagree

68. I often identify and eliminate things that cause stress.

Strongly agree   ○   ○   ○   ○   ○   strongly disagree

69. My position comes first and the other person follows in an argument.

Agree on   ○   ○   ○   ○   ○   Disagree

70. I work hard to emerge a winner when I face challenges.

Strongly Agree   ○   ○   ○   ○   ○   strongly Disagree

Calculating your score

When calculating your score, you look at the four models of emotions, which include the identification of emotions, using them, managing and manipulating them to solve problems situations. The score scale is 1to 5, and this depends on the question; if the answer to the question is strongly disagree, then strongly disagree begins the scale as 1 and strongly agree is at the end of the scale as 5. If the correct answer is agreed, then the agree starts the scale and the rest follows up to disagree, which is given a scale of 5. 1 represents 10 points, 2 represents 8 points, 3 represents 6, 4 represents 4 points, and 2 represents 2 points. This means that 1 is the highest score and 5 is the lowest score. Only the answers with the highest score will be given per question and the rest will be determined and calculated by the person who has done the test.

The questions tests skill on relationship management on the following aspects self-expression, judgment, sensitivity, self-control, openness, self-analysis, and analysis of others.

Questions on self-analysis the high scorers will often show that they are in touch with their emotions, as well as feelings, and therefore, they are always aware of the changes that occur when the experience certain emotions. The high scorers are those who get 8 and 10 points. The moderate scorers, on the other hand, their awareness of the changes in their mood is moderate and therefore, sometimes they are aware of the changes in their mood and sometimes they are not. The score range is 6 points. The low scorers are not aware of their emotions; they rarely pay attention to their emotions and feelings, and when they are experiencing emotions, they do not think about the causes or the effects.

When it comes to the analysis of others, the high scorers will easily identify the emotions and feelings of other people. They quickly sense the changes in the emotions of other people. The moderate scorers sometimes pay attention to the emotions and feelings of other people and sometimes identify when the emotions and feelings of other people change. The low scorers, on the other hand, pay little or no attention to the emotions and feelings of other people and show indifferent to what other people are feeling.

The other aspect of relationship management that is tested in the test is self-expression, which is how better you communicate your feeling to others. The high scorers in this aspect are highly skilled in describing their own emotions to others and communicating them, while the moderate scorers are moderate in describing their emotions and feelings to other people. The low scorers struggle to communicate their emotions and feelings, and therefore, they rarely share their feelings with other people.

When communicating with other people, you should easily tell when something is wrong, for instance when someone's smile is not genuine. The high scorers in this aspect are able to pick up emotional cues very easily to realize when there is deception or change in emotions. The moderate scorers are moderately competent in picking up emotional cues and realizing when things are not going right, and the low scorers have no idea if there are changes in the emotions when they are communicating with the other people. The low scorers, therefore, experience the changes when things are already out of hand and reacting to them is not possible.

The aspect of the use of emotions can be measured determining how a person thinks during a particular situation. The high scorers will often follow their feeling and allow them to give guidance on how they react to situations. For example, if your feelings let you concentrate on what is more important at the moment, then you are competent in using your feelings positively. The moderate scorers let their feelings guide them sometimes, while the low scorers prefer to use the incoming information about a situation instead of letting their feelings to guide them.

Chapter 7: The Art of Persuasion

Basics of persuasion

Persuasion is making people follow your idea or support you in doing something. This happens in arranged interactions such as business meetings, job interviews, and in daily social interactions. For persuasion to be effective the individual that is using this method must know some basics.

The topic of persuasion is very important as it determines the effort and tactics used in persuasion. If the topic is too complex for the audience, it might not be easy to convince them and therefore all the efforts available that seem effective can be employed to convince the audience. The topic might also be too complex for you as the persuader, and therefore, seeking help from the experts is always useful. It might not sound good when you give wrong information about something and expect people to believe you.

The age and level of education of the people you are talking to is also an important aspect to have in mind. This helps to choose the language and approach to use to persuade them; the method you use to persuade children is not the same as the one used to persuade adults or students in college. Also, experts in health cannot be persuaded using the same language as that used to persuade mothers who have little knowledge in the field of health.

Tools for persuasion which include facts and aids such as videos should be considered and their accessibility; you cannot use something you do not have, and therefore as you prepare for the persuasion always keep this in mind.

Methods of Persuasion

Reciprocation

The society operates on the principle that I give you back what you gave me. This can be in the form of behavior, favor or even something physical. For example, if I helped you when you needed help, when I need help you will help me as well. This is because, after I help you, you become obligated to do help me at a later time when I need it and not to the other person who did not help you. This method of persuasion works because the groups in the society that uses the principle of reciprocation are always competitive compared to the groups that do not use. Members of such a group will gladly give out resources because they know that it is a credit that will be paid back when the time comes. Therefore, when you are persuading people, master the skill of sharing or exchanging favors with the ones you intend to persuade and you will create a partnership that would enable you to get what you want from them.

Use of Scarcity

According to research the merit of something does not matter unless it is put in a context where it is required. Simply put, people will always be in need of what they cannot get at that time. When you have an idea, and what you are offering to the people is something that they can easily get it somewhere else, there is a likelihood that they will not listen to it and take it. Therefore, for a persuade to be effective in using this method, he or she should present arguments that have many advantages to make the other party realize that your idea is the one with more merits and move in your direction. Again, it is important to know that sometimes people are interested in what they would lose, because in some instance what one loses can be more valuable than what he or she is gaining. Therefore, it is also important to always good to explain on the losing side to persuade those who feel that they will lose the most important thing or part. However, to make sure that the negative side does not affect your persuasion, bring in new information to guide them to your side. There are people, who are quick to analyze situations, and it is not easy to convince them, always do your research well to make sure that they are not left out.

The Use of Authority

Most people trust information from the expert or from powerful people; if it is from the experts then it is true. This one becomes difficult because it is not always that a doctor will talk to people about health issues or a lawyer about legal matters, but you can always include them in your conversation to assure the people that what you are telling them is the knowledge that is approved by experts. If this is not possible you can use terminologies from the field of your topic and quote phrases or words spoken by experts in the field to establish the authority of your information.

Use of the Consistency

Persuasion is sometimes a process, and you must involve the people in the process up to a point that they feel that there is no way back. This is done during a discussion when decisions are made at each stage and there is no reversal of a decision that is made in the previous stage. The persuader can use a language such as, we can now count on you, right? The person agrees to the statement, and the next state is welcomed for discussion. The fact that they agreed in the previous stage prompts them to agree to what they are being asked regardless of what they feel about at that stage.

Use of Liking

People will always agree to follow the people they have a liking for, and dismiss the other person. Persuaders have known this behavior and mostly use it to their advantage. That is why most advertisements are done by famous and most like celebrities; the advertiser knows that if they like the person, they would tend to like the product that is associated with that personality. The thinking of the audience is that by using the product, you are part of the person advertising the product. The same idea can be used to support big ideas and programs.

The Use of Consensus

The consensus method uses the idea that if you get more people on your side, there is a possibility that the others will follow you. This method is used mostly used in parliament discussions; the idea that is supported by many people is endorsed and assumed that it is a decision that has been made by all the members of the parliament. Persuaders have known that if they get many people to their side not matter by what mean, their idea would easily be taken as acceptable by all and endorsed. The other group is therefore persuaded to join the large group.

The choice of method depends on many things such as the characteristics of the audience, the topic you are talking about, how much knowledge you know about the topic. Different methods can also be used in one situation; for instance, when politicians are persuading people, they can use reciprocation and consistency to let people agree with their idea and follow them. The most used method for small children is the use of the liking method; you can cover sweets with their best cartoon, and you will be sure that they will compel their parents to buy for them the sweets.

Body Language

When making a presentation in front of people and you need to establish the credibility of the information you are giving them so as to make an impression that would make them believe and take up what you are telling them. In addition, your aim might be to create a relationship with the people you are talking to. In this case, your body language must be in line with your words to create an impact on whoever you are speaking to. Most people look at the body language to determine how serious you are or how serious is the issue you are talking about, and in most cases, it affects their decision to follow what you are telling or not. In the case of a clash between your words and your body language, many people would follow your body language.

Therefore, you should make an effort to use your body language correctly to persuade people to believe or take up whatever you are telling them. First, you should make sure that the first impression you make to those you are persuading makes them connect with you. According to research, it takes only a few minutes of your first meeting to make an impression, and as you continue to interact, some of the people would have already made up their minds. When you meet people for the first time, face them directly, and like you, great them, give them a powerful smile as many people focus on your face to gauge your emotional state, attitude, and feelings. Looking directly at them shows interest in them, and they would be ready to listen to you. If there is something that has created tension between you and the other party, it is better to immediately show understanding by slightly tilting your head and nodding. Always be careful not to make a rigid face. Maintain a smile also creates a warm feeling and confidence between the two parties, thus establishing a rapport.

The first touch also has an impact; it can either be a cold or warm touch. In most cultures, when people meet for the first time, they touch through a handshake. A handshake is universally acceptable, and is done in social setting and business meetings; it is considered as safe. It conveys and brings about a warm feeling and friendliness. Therefore, it is good to keep your handshake brief and firm enough by applying only the required pressure and holding for less than 5 seconds. Most people dislike handshakes that are unwelcoming and show disinterest; such interests include cold fish handshake and finger or limp handshake, where only fingers tough briefly. The power play handshake that shows a dominating character, as well as the vise handshake, does not create a good impression, especially in the business meetings.

You should also adopt a posture that portrays openness; this also brings about a warm feeling and it is a sign of being receptive. Some people usually unbutton their coats before sitting down and sit forward moving closer to each other to show that they are relaxed and ready to listen to them.

The walking posture also has an effect on the way people might perceive you and later listen and agree to what you have to tell them. Walking upright shows that the person is confident and competent while walking with slumped shoulders shows that the person is not certain, ease and he or she is vulnerable. Some swing their hands s they walking quickly and briskly for them to appear s goal-oriented people.

During your conversation with the other party, it is important to maintain eye contact. It is logical that if you like someone, you will constantly give them a glance; it makes people know that they are appealing to you or you find what they are saying interesting. If you want to show people that you feel empathy, you can do it by looking at them directly in their eyes. Where people look during a conversation also determines the relationship the parties conversing have; it is easy to convince a person you show a good relationship with and vice Versa. When you show nervousness, it is obvious that you would not look the person directly into the eyes, which brings in a feeling of mistrust; a party that does not trust you would rarely give in to your persuasions.

The dressing is also part of the body language as it portrays the image of the person. More often people world judge others according to the clothes they have on. Without knowing, clothes we wear bring to light our deep personal values, as those who are seeing us connect with them consciously or unconsciously. For instance, if you put clothes that are considered conservative, people will give us such labels immediate they look at us. However, if you choose to be neat and smart, most people would immediately connect with you and therefore trust you. The clothes also bring out the impression of authority, and with the right clothes, one can easily create an impression of competence, authority, and professionalism. Doctors wear a white coat, and when you meet him or her in the white coat talking about healthy, it is likely that you will listen and believe him or her more than when in normal dressing. The same applies to business suits in the business world. In the normal social setting colors of the clothes take control with colors such as blue, charcoal grey and black showing more strength and competence. Therefore choose the right clothes and color to show authority and competence in whatever you are talking about.

Once you are now deep in the conversation with the other party, it is important to involving mirroring and pacing to make sure that the other party is following you. This is important to establish whether your persuasion has an impact, and if not you can slowly change your tactics to keep the other party on track. More often, when people have established a deep rapport, their body language synchronizes automatically, and this can be seen in their body posture. Their sitting posture will be somehow similar if they agree on whatever they are talking about, and similarly, if they fall out in their conversation, their body posture clashes. Although mirroring comes naturally, as a persuader, you should consciously use it to bring people on your side. For example, a good seller will establish a rapport with the buyer, but looking at the language of the buyer and his or her vocabulary use, the seller will slowly mirror the language of the buyer to make him or her knows that they are at the same level. In this case, the buyer and the seller will eventually agree on the same thing, which is to exchange the product and money. Mirroring can be done in other ways such as speech patterns and sitting or standing posture, however, you should be careful not to offend the other part because it might appear as mimicking.

Chapter 8: Making Friends

Human beings are often described as social beings. This means that we have several relationships with people in the world. These relationships have to lead to the rising of the creation of friends. A friend can be described as an individual who has a special bond or shares a mutual affection. Having friends is very important in the being of humans. An individual is supposed to know three components when making friends. An individual is advised to know types of friends how to make friends and importance of friends in their lives.

Types of Friends

1. Loyal best friend

There are several moments in life an individual can experience that is very heart aching. The set of a friend known as a best friend who is loyal will help an individual to remain sane during these moments. Everybody deserves to have a friend who will not judge him or her in complicated situations. These kinds of friends are always supportive of anything an individual decides to do. They let an individual get into a hot mess and still give a helping hand from problems. They know the deepest secret of somebody but still have the unconditional form of love for an individual.

2. Fearless with adventure

Despite the world being termed as the global village, there are several things in it. The world contains several activities being done, numerous people to be met and new experiences to be undertaken. Several people have programmed themselves to only operate their lives with their daily routine. This makes people forget several things that go on in the daily life apart from their routines. Therefore, this kind of friend has the role of taking people outside the shell they are used to. These friends are responsible for introducing an individual to new cultures activities ideas, philosophies.

3. Brutal open confidant

The normal life of a human being presents him or her with different situations. There are certain moments in life where an individual is accustomed to hearing the bitter truth. This role is tasked to a friend who is referred to as an as brutal open confidant. There are several situations that this kind of friend can manifest. A good example can be depicted in a relationship setting. If an individual has broke up and gets together with a loved one, for a period of five times, the situation can be described as normal by other people. However, the role of a brutal open friend in this situation is to tell a person to completely end the relationship. He or she goes ahead to tell an individual that he or she deserves better.

This can be an honest view that is honest from other people and it might be bitter to be done or heard. People are encouraged to have friends who are honest with them on every issue they face or think about. It is advisable to keep holding on to a relationship with an individual who is honest. These people are very rare to come by on this generation. In addition, these people offer a constructive form of honest.

4. Wise mentor

The common philosophy practiced by this kind of friend is to only look down on people on moments you are helping them. This kind of friend is very smart, intelligent and admirable. It is easy to change when this kind of friend is around you. The change process is easy because such a friend has the ability to motivate you when you are discouraged. They are a very important set of people in one's life because they help him or her to achieve a set of goals in life.

A wise mentor doesn't necessarily have to be an individual one shares with a hobby or occupation. Such a friend can be tuned to be several steps ahead of an individual. He or she also has a higher scale of patience and wisdom in life to be able to offer life guidance. This friend can either be a neighbor, a colleague, or somebody who is beyond one with years.

Despite these specifications, the person is supposed to be an individual you look upon in life.

5. One from a different culture

People in the modern generation are very inter-mixed. Therefore, an individual would not be in good terms being referred to as somebody who chose to stick to his or her own ways. The globe is better when people from different upbringings interact. Having a friend from a different social upbringing helps an individual to explore different values, traditions, and customs. There are several moments in life that an individual can adopt these new practices.

One is supposed to be careful in befriending people who are from different cultures. It is because people who are supposed to be befriended are those whom you click with. The next step is supposed to put in the effort to learning traditions values and customs as you get to know him or her on a personal level.

6. Polar opposite

People are designed in a very complicated way. It is very difficult for an individual to get along with someone who is of a different personality or character. The way we majorly operate is by teaming up with people who have the same view as us an attacking those who oppose it. However, there is a high chance that an individual will detach from the rest of the world if he or she only focuses on likeminded people. Therefore an individual can break free of the norm and associate with people who have opposing views. Having such a friend will help an individual to open his or her eyes to a different view of life. This kind of friend helps one to get closure of the opposing views he or she has.

7. Friendly neighbor

The modern form of living and housing structures has made people not know their neighbors. This phenomenon can be described as shameful. It is because there are certain neighbors who are very nice. Having such a friend can save an individual in certain occurrences in life. This is a friend who will help you pulling the key or locking the door when one forgot. A friendly neighbor can be very dependable people and are a breed worth dying for. However, one is not supposed to introduce him or herself to every person in a new neighborhood he or she goes to.

8. Work friend

It will shock several people who learn to know that they spend 50% of their time at work if they are self-employed. It is a common thing for people in the current world to think about their careers. This entails pays, overtime chances and career promotions that are often thought of. It is scientifically proven that an individual can be highly depressed when he or she is lonely at work. This makes it important for an individual to get a work friend who he or she can converse with. Such a friend can help a person to get through the week easily because it is easy to converse with them about work-related issues. The set of a work friend does not have to be one's best friend.

Steps of Making Friends

The process f making new friends look like an intimidating process. However, it is a very very rewarding act. It is because these friends we create in our day to day life tend to form a bigger part of life we leave. The help people share out their joy express their fears and reveal their pain. People who are seen to be swift in making friends, it is possible to find that at some point in their life, they were secluded people. However, the question that crosses people's minds is how they made it. There are several steps that an individual can use to make friends in his or her life. These steps include:

1. Realizing the fear in one's head

The first step an individual has to do is making sure that one has a good image mentally before meeting people. There are several people who see the event of meeting new people as scary. There are several things that cross an individual mind when making friends. People tend to focus on how well the conversation is going, if the person likes him or her and if one has made a good impression. These thoughts are what make the process scary when they are thought of continuously. Therefore, one is supposed to clear his or her head and keep his or her normal character.

2. Starting slowly with people a person is familiar with

It is difficult to jump in a zone of strangers when you have not been associating with people. This makes a need for using people one knows to help ease the process. This is a very easy task but it acts as a stepping stone. There are several groups of people that can start with. An individual can choose to reach out to acquaintances. He or she go-ahead to look for common groups he or she can join then proceed to know friends of the acquaintances and accepting invitations.

3. An individual getting out him or herself

This is the next step an individual can use after getting to know friends in his or her inner circle. An individual is supposed to get out extending his or her scope of people. The process can easily be done when a person joins several meets up groups, volunteers to several acts attend various workshops, becomes open to the online communities and visits socials places such as bars and clubs.

4. Being bold to take the first step

When one is used to having people around him or her, there is always a responsibility of will make the first move. A person is supposed to make the first move if the other party is delaying. The step can be simple since it starts with a "hello". During this time, a person can share something and give the other person an opportunity to share his or hers. It can be about how his or her day is faring.

5. Being open

The stage entails two critical aspects of making friends. The first aspect involves an individual having an open mind and not being judgmental. There is a set of friends an individual can choose to have who have the same thinking about life. However, a person is supposed to be open and give friendship time for its blossoming. It is because there are several good friends who can come from different backgrounds. The second aspect involves an individual opening his or her heart. This act involves trusting the goodness that can come from other people and believing in it. Opening the heart with good intentions often attract the same kind of people who reflect an individual.

6. Getting to know the other party

Friendship is a mutual issue therefore; both parties are supposed to know each other. Several questions such as where a person comes from, what he or she does, what he or values and what motivates him or her are cleared during the process.

7. Connecting with the other party genuinely

There are several factors that can make an individual lose the whole point of friendship. These factors are associated with an individual only thinking about him or herself. Concerns such as what will people think of me or what to say the net is supposed to be shunned away from. One can learn how to be presentable and know how to present his or her ideas. However, he or she is not supposed to be obsessed with them.

8. Being yourself

One is not supposed to change his or her character in order to make new friends. Therefore, an individual is supposed to be him or herself. It will give people who like you a chance to decide if they are willing to the relationship to the next level. Getting friends is attracting people who feel are compatible with your way of life.

9. Being there for him or her

Ideal for friendship is supposed to be a supportive union. A person is supposed to be there when he or she is able to offer help that is needed by a friend in need of it. This help can be returned later during the progression of life. Helping other people also offers a form of satisfaction.

10.   Have the effort of staying in touch

This is the crème of friendship. There needs to a constant form of communication to a person an individual has created as a fried. The process needs effort because it is important to maintaining a long-lasting form of friendship.

Chapter 9: Leadership

Leadership is a core factor in the current world. Because it is critical to managing people to make people work towards a common goal. Those people at the helm to manage people are given the task of leadership. This post of leadership is either vested in people or by wing support and trust from people.

Therefore, leadership can be described as the act in which one influences people to achieve a common set of goals. One is supposed to put the effort into interpersonal relationships for the process of influencing people to be successful. It is because people who are leaders commonly identify influence and achieving set objectives as common denominators.

Characteristics of Leadership

It is a continuous process of influence

Influence can be described as an individual being able to transform several aspects of people's lives. The common aspect that influences changes are believes the behavior and attitude of an individual. The transition experienced can either be directly or indirectly experienced. The process of influence enlists leadership as the process of social influence. The process supports or gives people aid in attaining a common set of goals.

Leadership is multi-dimensional

The most essential backbone of leadership is the attribute of followership. Therefore, leadership does not entail an individual having only one dimension on issues. The diverse and multi-dimensional comes into play when an individual employs his or her thinking system and organizational performance. The organizational performance involves people who are below him or her. This ideology makes leadership nonexistent if there are no followers.

Leadership have several facets

Leadership contains several aspects that are needed in the current world. The first set of combination includes personality and tangible skills. The tangible skill that is being talked about refers to self-drive, personal integrity, good personality, and self-confidence. These facets also include styles and situational factors. Styles trod from fair to authoritarian while situational factors include both internal and external factors.

Leadership is oriented on goals

The act of leadership entails organizing people to focus on the same aim. These set objectives are what influence is narrowed to achieving. Having the same goals that align is what also brings people together in the current world.

Leadership is not anchored on a specific personality trait

The world has been sometimes blinded to believe that leadership focuses only on one trait. The most common trait that is linked with leadership is known as charisma. However, charisma is a common trait that can be manifested by various people. The set of people that have this common character trait include sports heroes and movie actors yet they are not leaders.

Leadership does not have to be a formal position

The notion of leadership being associated with the high-end position is supposed to be withdrawn. It is because the world has witnessed several great leaders who did not hold high positions. One of the most famous leaders who brought enormous change without holding a position was Martin Luther King Jr. On the other hand, there are several people in the current world who hold high positions and are not leaders.

Leadership does not involve only set objectives

People who are under leaders have other things that want to be done collectively. Therefore, leadership entails getting other things done in the process of influencing people.

Leadership does not entail only a set of behaviors

There are several ideologies that can shift this principle involving leadership. They seem to equate leadership with delegating duties providing inspiration and giving motivations. These are actions that can be done by people who are not leaders. There are some of these attributes that are not done by effective leaders.

PRINCIPLES OF LEADERSHIP

For principles of leadership to come to light, there are several things a leader is supposed to do. These are the basic principles a leader is supposed to follow. They include:

1. Knowing oneself and always seeking to improve oneself

There several things an individual is supposed to know about him or herself when he or she is a leader. One is supposed to know his or her being and completely understand the attributes he or she poses. The process of seeking to improve oneself entails the constant strengthening of an individual's attributes. The process can be achieved through several things. This includes formal classes, self-study, interacting with other people and self-reflection.

2. Being technically proficient

This is one of the principles that signify leadership. An individual is supposed to be able to have a solid familiarity with the tasks of those below him or her. It goes a notch higher to a person understanding his or her roles.

3. Seeking responsibility and taking responsibility for one's actions

Leadership involves a person looking for several new ways that steer a group of people to more heights. When things tend to go wrong soon or later, a good leader does not blame those below him or her. The best course of action taken by leadership is to analyze the situation and then take corrective measures that are appropriate. When everything has been corrected, leaders are not afraid of taking on the next form of challenge.

4. Making decisions that are timely and sound

Leadership entails having a great ability to solve issues. It goes ahead to demanding for an individual who can clearly make decisions that are accurate and have good ability to plan for the future.

5. The setting of a good example

A leader is supposed to be a good example to emulated by his or her followers. People below an individual are not supposed to only hear about what they must do. A good precedent is shown to be actions from the seniors. Leaders are supposed to be the change they desire to be seen in other people.

6. Knowing out of one's followers and constantly looking out for their well being

Good forms of leaders are people who are constantly updated with human nature. Leadership also provides the need for an individual to sincerely care for the people who are below him.

7. Keeping everyone constantly informed

A great form of leadership involves a person who is a good communicator. A leader is supposed to know how to communicate and keep his followers constantly informed. The individual is supposed to also suppose to be able to communicate to the superiors or those above him or her.

8. Developing a sense of responsibility to those people who are below him or her

The process of leadership is transformative. The process is supposed to develop good character traits in people. This is a role that is tasked with a leader who is at the helm. These traits are supposed to be efficient and effective when an individual is tasked with the role of achieving certain communal goals.

9. Ensures that the roles given are understood, supervised and done to completion

This principle is well achieved when a leader is a good communicator.

10. Training as a team

There are several heads who call those below them a team. However, this might not be the case because of how they handle the group. Leadership entails moving and doing things as a group. This helps to cover the weaknesses and strengths of other people. This helps people to accomplish their tasks and goals easily.

11. Using the full capabilities of one's followers

By having a team it is easy to accomplish this principle. After understanding the weakness and strength of those below one, he or she can be able to delegate tasks to these people according to their strengths. He or she can then improve the weakness of his or her followers. This helps to obtain maximum utility of those below an individual.

ADVANTAGES OF LEADERSHIP

A strong leader can help a group of people to break through their set out goals. These people help others to flourish. On the other hand, a poor set of leaders is related to the failure of achieving goals by those they lead. The process of managing people focuses keenly on leadership. Good leadership accelerates effectiveness and efficiency when managing people to attain common goals. The advantages of leadership are myriad. They include:

1. He or she inspires and guides the juniors

A leader helps in providing supervision to those people who are below him. This process of supervision comes in handy with guiding people who are below him or her. In this context, guidance entails a leader instructing those who are below him to perform their duties in a manner that is efficient and effective. This helps to create a sense of belonging to those who are under an individual. It also helps to bring an improved sense of commitment from people. Therefore, people are able to convert their desires to achieve passion.

2. Secures co-operation from people

Leadership is an act that sells and does not tells. While other people tend to dictate, a great form of leadership persuades people. This helps to create enthusiasm when working toward a common aim among people. Such an act helps people to gain immense co-operation from people.

3. Helps to create confidence

In the world we leave in, confidence is a very important factor. It is achieved when an individual expresses his or her efforts while doing the job to his or her followers. It entails giving people clear roles and guided lines to work within an efficient and effective manner. This helps people to achieve goals in a more fast way. Confidence also involves hearing and addressing complaints that are made by people an individual leads.

4. Builds a good working environment

The process of management is proving to be critical in helping people to get the thing done. A good environment is a great breeding ground for growth and development. Therefore, a good leader is supposed to keep in mind the power of good relations. He or she is supposed to be in consistent communication with people hearing them out. When these people have a problem, he or she is supposed to be able to provide them with solutions. Leadership creates a conducive working environment because people are treated with humanitarian terms.

5. Aids in maintaining discipline

Securing compliance and order from people becomes an easy task for an individual. The process is only described as easy when he or she has turned those below him or her to be followers. The process can be done by motivating employees using rewards. The rewards can be economic or noneconomic. This helps to get those under him or her to work involuntarily manner to achieve set out goals. Therefore, willingness is the first set a leadership provides to help maintain discipline among people.

6. It helps to facilitate the integration of group goals and personal goals

A leader is a visionary person who is tasked with the ability to decide on the destination to be reached. The vision of goals provided by a set of people is supposed to be well synchronized with their personal objectives. A leader is tasked with the role of helping people below him or her gets the synchronicity of goals in both their private and group goals. This also promotes a sense of belonging among people. It is a key factor in enhancing coordination between people.

7. It has the ability to work as a transformation agent

There is no change that can be witnessed only by thinking. It is important for people to release that the process and practices of change are successful when people have a good leadership system. It is a leader who helps to change people and influence their thoughts and actions. This helps to create a path that has the least resistant to the desired change.

8. It boosts people morale

Boosting of people morale moral can be described as the act of a leader making sure that his or her followers have the confidence of achieving their goals. Leadership helps people to be psyched up to performing their roles to attain the objectives.

Leadership Issues in the Contemporary World

The eye that has been focused on leadership in the current world is strong. There some issues about leadership that has been clearly been brought to light. They include:

1. Emotional intelligence

A good leader is supposed to have high levels of intelligence quotient and also have high levels of technical intelligence. These two aspects are critical however; it is also important for a leader to poses high levels of emotional intelligence. There are five components that determine an individual emotional quotient. These components include good social skills, great levels of empathy, being self-motivated, being self-regulated and being self-aware. It proves to be difficult for an individual to become a leader without these five components of emotional intelligence. The recent years have seen Nooyi Indiria become the president of one of the largest companies in the world know as Pepsi because she had high emotional intelligence.

2. Gender and leadership

The question that lingers in people's minds when the topic is raised is if gender is important in leadership. Several leader participation models have found out that leaders who are women have a unique quality. The unique quality portrayed by women leaders more than men leaders is the attribute of being more participatory. These set of leaders are very interactive to their followers. This is what gives them a high rating from people who work under and above them.

Leadership is supposed to give a chance to every gender in the world. Therefore, every gender is supposed to be given a chance and motivation to take the mantle.

3. Cross-cultural leadership

The recent times have seen the world becoming a village because of advancements in transport and communication sectors. Several organizations across the globe have been identified by appointing expatriates. Companies such as Vodacom have employed people from various social backgrounds and countries. Such a company has gone to a different millage of sending its workers to different companies to work from there. The best case that can elucidate this case is their former employer known as Bob Collymore. He was a man from the Carrabin Islands, he grew up in Britain and he was sent to Kenya during his last assignment.

There is an important reason that supports these acts by multinational companies. The main important reason is to reduce the cultural shock that is caused by interacting with new people. On the other side, culture plays an important role in and therefore those who are tasked with leadership are supposed to understand other people's cultures. The world has also seen elected leaders of having different backgrounds holding high offices because of their expertise. The best example is Mr. Barack Obama who is the former president of the United States of America.

4. Building trust

There are several leaders in the past and in the present general who are corrupt and are not accountable. These incidences are known to the public because of the power in technology in communication. Such activities have the biggest potential to demeaning trust that is bestowed to leaders by those they call followers. High trust involves a leader who is open, loyal, consistent and impeccable integrity levels. This is what the current world refers to as an ethical form of leadership.

Chapter 10: How to Be a Good Storyteller

There are people who love telling stories even though they may not know how to make their stories interesting to the listeners. People are interested in able to tell it when the storyteller is good. They will tell it through the way an introduction is done. As much as there are good storytellers, there are also bad and boring storytellers. However, it is important to ensure that you have good storylines that will capture the interests of the audience.

When you are a poor storyteller, you are likely to lose your audience. This is because they easily lose interest in your stories as they are not catchy enough to keep you listening. Did you know that the best way to engage people by giving stories? It can be in a presentation or a meeting. A good storyteller must own certain abilities. Any person may tell a story that was narrated to them by others. But one to be a distinguished storyteller must be able to do it repeatedly and in an interesting way.

He must be able to create the story afresh each time he narrates it. This makes it memorable and gives a meaningful experience for each audience. The success of any story depends on how it is narrated. When narrating a story the narrator has to give an explanation or give the meaning of any unfamiliar word that he happens to use.

A good storyteller performs many functions. He becomes the performer and a teacher as well as a social observer and a comedian too. He plays each role depending on the needs of the audience. This is because different stories are narrated to different audiences.

There is a story that is narrated to children, others are narrated to teens while there are those that are narrated to adults. If for instance, he is performing for children he will use simple and clear language and any other devices that the children will find entertaining.

The narrator will have to use the Imitation of speech from different characters in the story. For instance, telling a story about the hare, he will need to imitate characters and gestures comically as per the story. This will help in making the children entertained throughout the storytelling session. The storyteller should, therefore, look for relevant stories for each age group. A one to succeed in being a good storyteller, he or she must possess the below abilities.

Interested in Culture

A good storyteller is usually a person who is interested in the culture of his people. He has all the information about his culture. He has pride in his culture. He enjoys the richness of his language and knows its idioms and the figure of speech used.

Always Pleasant

He is always a pleasant person who enjoys entertaining the audience and is happy to pass the knowledge he possesses to others.

Have a Good Memory

A good narrator has a good imagination, is creative and has a good memory. A good memory will help in ensuring that they remember all incidences they are about to narrate well. This will help a lot in the flow of the story.

Be Open-Minded

An open-minded person should not be shy or timid. This is because he has to use some obscene words which cannot be unavoidable during narration. He is an actor who gestures with his hands and other parts of the body. The narrator's open-mindedness will enable them to be able to welcome any ideas about bettering their narrations without hesitating.

Keen Observer

He does not only knows the past but also a keen observer of what is happening today and able to comment on the conditions. He acts as a bridge between the world of yesterday and today.

How do You Tell a Good Story?

Have a Hook

As a storyteller, it is important to ensure that you hold the interest of your audience. This means that you need to get their interest first and that is what we call having a hook. You will be able to do this by ensuring that the start of the story is interesting. This will help in ensuring that you catch the interest of the storyteller from the start of the story. When starting the story, you should ensure that you give clues of what the story is about. As the story unfolds, the storyteller should keep giving leads on how the story will end which will help to keep the storyteller interested throughout the story.

By giving the audience a sense of what the story is about, they will not get lost. How you introduce the story will determine whether the audience will continue listening to you or not. Any time a storyteller starts a story and the audience doesn't seem interested, it is advisable to ensure that you look for ways to keep them interested.

Having a Point to the Story

Before you even start giving the story, it would be important to ask yourself if the audience needs to actually listen to you. Asking yourself that question will help you to decide whether you need to continue giving the story or not. It may give you a reason for looking for a better topic that will be more interesting to the audience. It is by asking yourself that question that you will be able to know if you should change the goal of the story or not. A storyteller should make sure that they package their story in such a way that it only contains the details which will support the goal of the story.

For you to keep the flow of the story, make sure that at the point where people need to laugh they laugh. They should also show sadness when your intention is to make them feel sad. This will enable you to be able to keep them connected to the story. It will not be necessary to give details that are not necessary to the story. When the flow of the story is good, you will be able to have an easy time connecting with the audience. This will also help you as a storyteller to be able to conclude your story when they least expect it. By doing this, it means that they will be left in suspense which will leave them wanting to hear more of your stories. However, the audience will want to hear more of your stories when they are able to connect with you from the start of the story to the end

Choosing the Most Appropriate Time to Tell the Story

A storyteller should be in a position to tell the right story at the right time. This will help in ensuring that the audience listens to you uninterrupted to the end. The story you choose to tell should always fit people's mood at a particular time. When people around you are sharing their funny stories, you should come up with a story that relates to their happy tales. When they are discussing tragedies, you should come up with stories about stories that are related to that topic. It wouldn't be wise to tell happy stories in when people's mood is sad. They may not even listen to you since their focus is on other things.

A good storyteller should also be in a position to relate the story to the situation at hand. When they are traveling, they should be able to tell a story related to traveling. This will make the story relevant to the current situation which will make the listeners connect with everything that is happening in the story. It is also important for a storyteller to make sure that the context of the story is one that is well understood by the audience. They can do this by giving a little background about the story they are about to narrate especially if the listeners are not aware of the characters in the story.

A good storyteller should be observant. They should interact with the people around them in order for them to identify other good storytellers among them. This will help them to share ideas on coming up with good stories. Through the ideas, they will be able to find their strengths and weaknesses. They will, therefore, work on their weaknesses which will help them to become better storytellers.

Making the Stories to Sound Real

Most people will be interested in your stories if they sound real. They will be able to relate them to real life. A good storyteller should be in a position to make the audience to imagine the scenes as if they were real. When they do this, they will be able to deeply connect with the story and will keep remembering the story even after listening to it.

A good storyteller should also be able to able to dramatize some of the scenes in the story. They should only dramatize the necessary parts in order to avoid overdoing it. Overdoing the scenes may make the narration boring hence the need to avoid them. When narrating a story about how you were attacked by the shark in the ocean, you do not need to show how you were attacked but rather how you fought back. This will make the story interesting since everyone in the audience will be keenly following to see the dramatic scene of how you fought the shark.

A good storyteller should also avoid repeating himself. Repeating details makes the audience to get bored. They may be tempted to stop listening to you and switch to other things. The trick is to make the audience interested in your story so just give details once and move to other new details.

Give More Facts and Fewer Details

Too many details bore the audience. Sometimes it would be better to give a simple description of how events unfolded. The audience will be keen to capture all the details than when you keep giving long stories.

They will be able to flow with the narration when you are precise and straight to the point. For the listeners to keep the interest in the story, you should be able to give vivid details which the audience will keep in their minds all along. They will flow with you as they imagine the scenes. This is because vivid scenes are interesting and at the same time surprising. The vivid details are also said to relate to the stories. The vivid details are also said to help a reader to imagine the scenes as if they were happening at that particular time. It is therefore important to ensure that as a storyteller, you give the readers more facts and fewer details.

Ensure that You Practice Related Skills

We all know that the best way to practice storytelling is by doing it in your day to day conversations.

However, one can still device better ways of doing so. A storyteller should ensure that they read as many storytelling books as possible. This will help them to be able to learn new storytelling skills which enables them to become better storytellers. A storyteller should also be able to identify the stories that interest them. This will make it easy for them to have a good flow in their story since they are comfortable with the topics they have chosen.

A storyteller will be able to tell that they have sharpened their skills when they keep their audience entertained throughout their stories. In actual performance, the audience is very important. The audience acts as a catalyst for the artist. A storyteller will be able to tell that they have succeeded in their storytelling journey when;

They Can Describe a Character or a Scene in an Interesting Way: You can give a vivid description of a character depending on the way the character behaves. This will make the audience to create mental pictures based on the description either in terms of character or scene. The use of some characters can be symbolic.

You Achieve a Good Flow in Your Story: Telling a story is not an easy task. It is with more practice that you master the art of storytelling. The more you write stories, the more creative you become. You will term yourself to be successful when you are able to narrate stories with a good flow and which the audience connects with. Once you own the stories, you will be able to narrate them comfortably. You will also be able to deliver the required message and which the audience can relate with.

Incorporate a Personal Story or a Song in Your Narration: A storyteller needs to be a person who can read people's moods when they are listening to their story. They should, therefore, make their stories interesting enough by including nice songs in their narration. They can also incorporate a personal story which is helpful in breaking the boredom. The personal story should be in relation to the narration. This will be of great help to the audience who sit for long hours doing the same thing. It may be so boring doing the same thing for long hours. A storyteller should, therefore, devise ways of making sure that the audience keeps listening to them. So, if your personal experience is captivating share it. If you don't have one look for a song that will suit whatever was being discussed. This will break the monotony and make the audience to join you in the song.

Merging With the Recent Events: Talking about stale things can be boring more so with the current generation. The only way could be merging what you were saying to what takes place in the current society. This will involve them and will participate actively. Through their participation, they get to understand the stories and even retell them to other people in the future. You will, therefore, have succeeded in maintaining the audience so at no time will you lack an audience to listen or read your stories. The audience will even recruit other members who may also start listening and also reading your stories. There is no greater motivation than a growing audience. It gives you the morale to research ways of giving better stories in order for you to keep your audience. This also benefits you since you sharpen your skills so you do not remain the same.

Use Provocative Questions: A good storyteller should be in a position to use provocative questions when there is a need. Provocative questions are important since they keep the audience interested. They will keep listening to you. It also helps in making sure that they are fully involved in the storytelling session. The audience must listen actively in order for them to answer the questions correctly. It also helps them not to get bored. They are expected to stay awake which makes them follow the story keenly. Using provocative questions is therefore very important and using them as a storyteller helps the audience to follow the story and also understand it.

Conclusion

Thank you for making it through to the end of *improve your social skills*, let's hope it was informative and able to provide you with all of the tools you need to achieve your goals whatever they may be.

The next step is to put the things learned to practice. One learns what social skills are. Most of the people never asked or answered that question but at the very end of this book has answered that. One also sees the importance of socials skills in our daily living. We also see if the social skills are in someone or they are acquired. There is also the fact that social skills differ from one person to another and then we can easily know how to work on them. As always, the difference in social skills makes our relation to people different.

The book also talks about emotional quotient and how to use it to your advantage. The meaning of emotional quotient has been looked at keenly. There also talks of self-awareness and all its techniques. There is also the self-management and all its aspects. There is also all about social awareness this is related to social skills and one must understand the aspects of social skills. There is also the point of making oneself better when you feel not so great and finally, there are practical examples that were listed to show these aspects in a more vivid form.

While interacting with others stress is bound to take over once in a while. That means one has to look for relieves. This book gave the ticket way to that. Those are things one should practice and also gave one phobia associated fear of being social. There is the talk of mindfulness and how one could improve. There is also the social phobia and all of the aspects concerning it. There is also setting the right mindset of the things one does. This may be positive or negative that depends on the person himself or herself. Also, assertiveness is key and was looked into.

The other thing discussed is emotional intelligence. In this what was looked into was the meaning of emotional intelligence. There is also the use of emotional quotient to deal with one's need. The uses were explained very keenly. There is also the intelligence scale and everything about it has been discussed. Therefor types of questions all discussed. There are types of aspects they use in the questions. It is one important thing in terms of emotional intelligence and the quotient in general. All have been discussed to the brim in the wonderful you just read.

Finally, there was an assessment of emotional intelligence. There instructions for the self – assessment. There is also the relationship management seen. Also the way of calculating the emotional intelligence score. There is also the art of persuasion. There are the basics of it and the methods of persuasion. The body language is also very key. Also, things like making friends have been looked at. Leadership is also key in this book so it has been seen through and finally, one is taught how to be a great storyteller. This is to avoid someone being bored with you while you are talking.

Finally, if you found this book useful in any way, a review on Amazon is always appreciated!